MW01234216

Published by
RDJ Publishing, LLC.

Library of Congress Cataloging in Publication Data

Jacobs, Raymond Douglas
        The Twenty Rhymes of Love and Reason / by R. Douglas
Jacobs
                        1v.
        TXu-1-214-260   2004

Jacobs, Raymond Douglas
        The Rhymes of Love and Reason / by R. Douglas Jacobs
                        1v.
        TXu-1-319-804   2006

        ISBN-13: 978-0-9789274-0-0 (hardcover)
        ISBN-10: 0-9789274-0-0 (hardcover)

Cover Art by Travis Cota
Original paintings and photography by Travis Cota
Additional photography by Ramon Caballero
Cover and production design by Tanja Richter

Printed in the United States of America

To my beloved Mother,
        For without whom I am nothing.

Words only tell of the meaning....

TABLE OF CONTENTS

SELF-PORTRAIT

I am the anomaly of a man,
One whose destiny in life began
When my innate gift for verse
Was first able to immerse
My mind with a sort of nuance
That became a renaissance
For which I could boldly explore
The meaning of each metaphor
With words that had the agility
To hone all degree of sensibility
So that the ink of my blood could reveal
A subliminal pain I still feel
Whenever the attitudes of men
Confine me to the remedy of my pen.

-R. Douglas Jacobs
November, 2004

HER MAIDEN PASSING

Dear be the thought I most covet

The one of you, my beloved

Or so I have often hoped

Amid a whim that my heart could elope;

Wanting like never before

A chance to love you evermore;

I make heed of this plea,

Of the passion I have for thee,

Knowing that I could never be your lover

While your touch be wed to that of another;

Still, your flawless beauty is to blame

For allowing my heart to languish in pain

Over the mere notion of what could have been

Had it been I instead of him.

-R. Douglas Jacobs
March, 1997

THE CRADLE OF LIFE

The existence of life dwells
On the parallel of heaven and hell;
The axis of love and hate
That is equated by a fate
Of what is misunderstood
Amid the perception of bad and good;
For the journey of the soul
Is merely virtual
To the clairvoyant eye
That detects age as an innate disguise
Resonating from the womb
A calling for innocence that entombs
The secular nature of birth
With the soil of the earth.

-R. Douglas Jacobs
November, 2001

IF ONLY

If only you were to ask
Could I then accept the task
Of being the one who would assume
A role that others have impugned
So that your impulsive demands
Could be humbled by another that commands
The sheer sense of your devotion
With an enchanted notion
That cannot be likened to anything
Since the love that you bring
Yearns ever so deeply, if only to beckon
In ways that are bound to reckon
A longing that has always cried
For the very promise my heart can provide.

-R. Douglas Jacobs
January, 2004

BIAS PRUDENCE

If I had only one wish
Would it be to replenish
The sum of my existence
With an absolute sense
Of unconditional love
That could soar above
The extent of my sorrow
With the hope of tomorrow
So that I may forgive those
Whose antipathy is to impose
A prejudice without virtue
That has and will continue
To be the unyielding source
Of a life full of remorse.

-R. Douglas Jacobs
September, 2002

THE SILENCE OF HADES

If this be the eulogy of my story

Than sing unto thee what ode of glory

May summon the voices of virtue,

Spoken by the chosen, yet noble few

Who leave nothing to be said

Of the silence that condemns the dead;

For innocence is but an enigma

Which encumbers the soul with stigma

That life answers for in time

When redemption is but a tacit rhyme

Beholding unto temptation's wake

A testament that sin could forsake

If fate, within the solace of peace,

Were to bless my legacy among the decease.

-R. Douglas Jacobs
April, 2000

DE FACTO

To solve the riddle of affliction
Is to know fact from fiction
Without relying on a clichè
To answer for the errors of our way;
For the truth can only take shape
If we are willing to escape
All that we have come to know
In having watched ourselves grow
Into the sort of individuals
Who rely on the pompous rituals
Of a secular dominion
In order to form a basis of opinion
That fails to assuage
The fears that come with age.

-R. Douglas Jacobs
April, 2000

HER FLOWERBED

Had my plot been soiled with thirst
The instant her flower burst
One mystically sublime eve
As I lay on her bed of potpourri;
For my lungs could not resist
The herbal scent of her mist
That doused the petals on my lap
With the luscious dew of her sap,
Glistening the limbs of her soul
Like some unearthly follicle
That had yet to fawn
The air amid the light of dawn
That the laws of nature would condemn
Had I not planted the seed to her stem.

-R. Douglas Jacobs
April, 2000

DENOMINATION

If life were to begin
Without the burden of sin,
By what end or cost
Could a soul be lost
If the laws of society
Continue to honor a deity
In the form of wealth?
For faith is too stealth
To assume the given path
Of any human epitaph
When the temptation of success
Matters more to those with less
Than the few whose deeds defy
Our need to question why.

-R. Douglas Jacobs
July, 2001

BECAUSE YOU ARE

You are my one and only
Whenever I am lonely,
You are the touch that fashions
The fabric of my passion,
You are the pure reflection
Of my most intimate affection;
You are the soul of my emotion
That is as vast as the ocean,
You are the life that is hallow
With each step that I follow,
You are the hope that redeems
My genuine sense of esteem,
You are the muse of my heart
My lasting perception of art.

-R. Douglas Jacobs
January, 2000

THE TALE OF A SONGBIRD

Second Edition

Lost is the fable of a wandering lark
Who finds her safe haven in the dark
For desires that are seldom known
Among those who have flown
Before the first sight of dawn;
For her hymn has come to spawn
An uninhibited air of mystique
That makes her evermore unique
Whenever the ambiance of the sky
Summons her to fly
To a place beyond the divide
Where all matter of nature collides
Under the constant weight that clings
Beneath the span of her wings.

-R. Douglas Jacobs
March, 2004

THE NAKED TRUTH

The nights I lay unwanted
Are when I feel most haunted
By the melancholy effect
Of human neglect
Which eclipses my senses
With the dire consequences
That fate holds in store
Should love continue to ignore
That which has come to bemoan
The very notion of being alone
Until I have neither the hope
Nor will to somehow cope
With a world that left behind
The life I had in mind.

-R. Douglas Jacobs
March, 2003

A PERSIAN KISS

Tempt thee by choice

With thou lips so moist

So that I may come to savor

The sweet and luscious flavor

That envelops your essence

With a warm succulence

That nurtures your kiss

During moments as tender as this

When words, alone, cannot convey

What it is we mean to say

In consummating a bond

That has transcended well beyond

The spoils that our lips feel

In quenching the thirst of our zeal.

-R. Douglas Jacobs
May, 1997

Dedicated to Bousse Ershadi

QUESTIONS

Why do we usually pretend
If only to befriend?
Why do we always boast
Over that which matters most?
Why do we take heed
For the sake of our own greed?
Why do we become enchanted
With what it is we take for granted?
Why do we so willingly lie
Only when certain matters go awry?
Why do we easily begrudge
Those whose lives we come to judge?
Why do we often doubt
In relation to all that we are about?

-R. Douglas Jacobs
June, 2006

L O V E

Say unto me so that my heart may hear

The spoken word it has come to revere

Without purpose, or without end

Whenever your voice begins to transcend

The mere nature of its sound

Into an idiom that is profound

In conveying the sort of sentiment

That is fondly meant

To seize my emotion

With an intrepid sense of devotion

So that the masculine

Impulse of what I imagine

May embody a significance beget

Within the context of each alphabet.

-R. Douglas Jacobs
October, 2006

EDEN

Cursed are we to defy that which is sacred

Since it is in our nature to stand naked

Before the throes of our chastity

Given how the gravity

Of temptation is inherent

In all things that are errant

Each time we entrust

The incarnation of our lust

To reap the fruit of one's decree

From the branch of a chastised tree

So that the dreams we desire

May live to aspire

The comfort of being awaken

In a paradise long forsaken.

-R. Douglas Jacobs
December, 2005

ELEGY

Let our lack of faith speak

For the fact that we are weak

In overcoming our penchant for sin

With an abiding discipline

That our spirit requires

If we hope to allay our desires

To better understand how our mortality

Is nothing more than a formality

That puts into sober perspective

The manner in which we all live

So that the transgressions of our past

May exist in stark contrast

To the life that is to follow death

Beyond our last gasp of breath.

-R. Douglas Jacobs
February, 2005

MILVIAN BRIDGE

Born were we of this moment in time
When the angst of fallen began to chime
Of the salvation they were denied
Once the fate of their allegiance died
Under the blade of an epiphany unseen
To all but the emperor Constantine;
Who, but for the might of his sword,
Ordained the initials of the Lord
Into the cast iron of his shield
So that the force with which he could wield
Would no longer be able to rescind
The transcendent nature of the wind
That resonates amid the unbridled North flank
Of her brisk, yet ancient riverbank.

-R. Douglas Jacobs
May, 2006

SIRENS

Amid the passing of each wave
Come tidings we must brave
If the legacies of the seven seas
Are to weather the incessant subtleties
That engulfs each thunderous swell
With aquatic sounds that parallel
The incantation of our gift
So that the souls which sail adrift
May follow the transient echoes
That led the mythic heroes
Of yesteryear, and lore
Along a voyage that knows no shore
Once their hearts became remiss
Over the fathoms of their own abyss.

-R. Douglas Jacobs
July, 2006

MINDSET

Life can be particularly hard
If we fail to disregard
The kind of subtle gestures
That serves to fester
Confusion like a cancer
Given that our search for answers
Often leaves us out of sync
With our ability to think
In a way that is meant
To make us evermore dependent
On the standards that constitute
A logic in which we all follow suit
Once the state of our humanity
Ceases to question its own sanity.

-R. Douglas Jacobs
September, 2005

THE OTHER FOOT

Would it be anything like before
If I were to look upon you once more
Knowing all that I know now?
For I often ask how
It was that I never saw
Even the slightest flaw
In thinking back on your behavior;
Maybe it was the thought of you as my savior,
Given my many moments of despair,
That made me completely unaware
Of what your true intentions were,
But seeing you with her
Cannot help but make me question
The folly of my own discretion.

-R. Douglas Jacobs
October, 2003

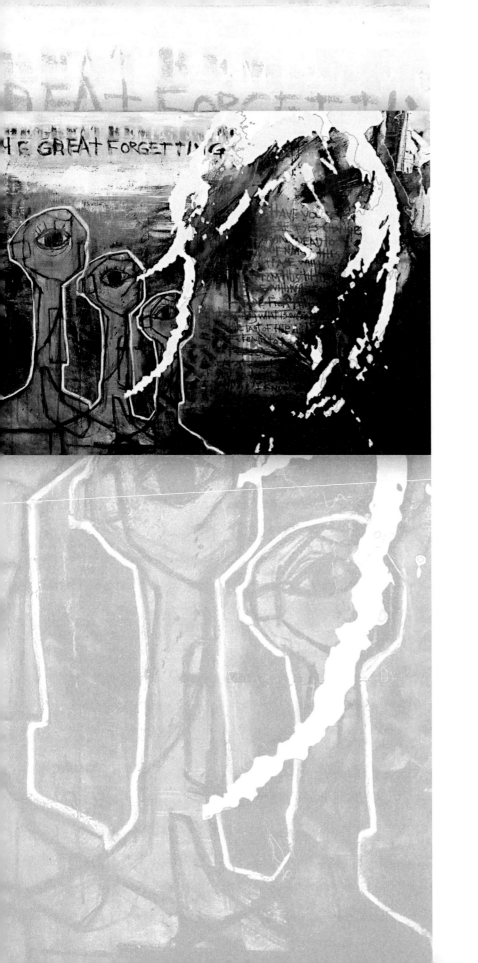

THE GREAT FORGETTING

THEM

Those who I often refer to as them
Live with a tendency to condemn
Someone of my uncanny stature
Given that my appearance is a departure
From the social norms that govern
What it is they so willfully discern
In judging one person from the next;
And, yet, in ignoring the ethical context
Of how I have managed to survive
Did my peers collectively arrive
At a hasty decision that subscribes
To the doctrine of their own tribe
In order to justify the ridicule
That demeans me in the role of a fool.

-R. Douglas Jacobs
January, 2005

A FORCE OF HABIT

Our inclination is to often wonder
Of the opportunities we squander
Whenever the failure of a hyperbole
Overshadows our psyche
With a feeling of distress
That causes us to second guess
The decisions we make
As ones we could just as well forsake
If we were not so naive
In being willing to believe
That the life we so yearn
Should not be of our own concern
Unless we are able to live in haste
For a mind we would no sooner waste.

-R. Douglas Jacobs
November, 2005

LUST

The touch that lingers

Beneath the tips of my fingers

Is one that longs to caress

The contours of your finesse

In a manner that would exude

The comfort of our interlude

With the kind of sensuality

That would mold our duality

With the sweat we perspire,

Once the logic of our desire

Has been intimately spent

Allowing our flesh to lament

Upon the ageless feeling

We embody with another being.

-R. Douglas Jacobs
April, 2004

CHECKMATE

How is it that I have the will

To love you as I do still

When the bonds of our affinity

Has yet to share the divinity

Of intimacy that is defined

The moment our hearts are entwined?

For the mere thought of this fact

Is a testament of my failure to act

Whenever the warmth of your smile

Inspires my heart to reconcile

The feelings I have longed possess

Yet, dare to confess

Out of fear that I may not be

The one you deem as He.

-R. Douglas Jacobs
October, 2004

A JESTER'S WALTZ

It is for no just cause
That I dance without applause
Among those of you who are immune
To the melodic beat of a tune
That accompanies my every stride
Once the tempo of my pride
Reaches its humble crescendo
Amid a movement of innuendo
That mocks the prowess of my routine
As one that is merely obscene
To the elite impression
Which begs to question
Whether my exercise in calamity
Can ever be misconstrued as vanity.

-R. Douglas Jacobs
February, 2006

THE IDOLATRY OF LOVE

If our passion is to endure
Than baptize me with the allure
Of your immaculate finesse
For I can feel the tenderness
Of your touch resurrect
My heart in every true aspect
So that the litany of my grief
May be absolved in a belief
That exists within a communion
For which the bonds of our union
Serve as but a smidgen
In ordaining love like no religion
Once the evocation of our lips
Are joined together in worship.

-R. Douglas Jacobs
August, 2005

SEMANTICS

The act of being alive

Is one that is often contrived

With adverbs that commence

The start of each sentence

For the sake of conjecture

Given how our need to lecture

Others of our logic

Is merely symbolic

In the pretext of expressing a theme

That is but a grand scheme

To render life to the contrary

Once the exploits of our vocabulary

Begins to articulate

The words that define our fate.

-R. Douglas Jacobs
January, 2006

A BEAUTY OF VISION

Your beauty is the incision
By which my heart has vision,
Leading me by the hand
Without motive or demand
While anointing my eyes with elation,
A bold sense of anticipation
I once felt as a mother's child,
Wanting to escape among the wild
And endure beyond measure
All the joy that comes with pleasure
That no passing, nor fateful hour,
Could ever defy or empower
Once your splendor as a whole
Has engendered my very soul.

-R. Douglas Jacobs
March, 2000

Dedicated to Blerime Topalli

EXISTENTIAL ECHOES

Be that it may, be that it may,
That the trials of each day
Can enable us to still live
In a way that can forgive
The past of our many faults
Which burden us as adults;
For, though, our times of yore
Come to serve as a metaphor
Of how not to judge, but behave,
The lessons that we save
Are but a reminder of the pain
That will always remain
Until the annuls of time
Ceases to become a paradigm.

-R. Douglas Jacobs
May, 2003

WHEN CUPID BLUSHED

Second Edition

Bedazzling to us are instances
In where appearances
Of love suddenly emerge
Igniting a compulsive urge
That acutely cajoles
The wistful nature of our souls
In ways that firmly enslave
A look that another gave
With an awe that ineffably
Molds our fleeting glimpse of ecstasy
Into something that puts into motion
The sheer, yet disarming notion
We behold for the mere thrill
Of feeling time stand still.

-R. Douglas Jacobs
August, 2006

HER MOSAIC AT DAWN

This morning when I awoke

Did my first glimpse of her evoke

An effervescent blur

That began to transfigure

The silhouette of her face

Under a plethora of space

That emanated like twilight

For but a moment until my sight

Was suddenly restored,

Leaving me in awe, while I adored

The manner is which her slumber

Had come to encumber

An aura that could only be defined

By an immaculate ray of sunshine.

-R. Douglas Jacobs
July, 2002

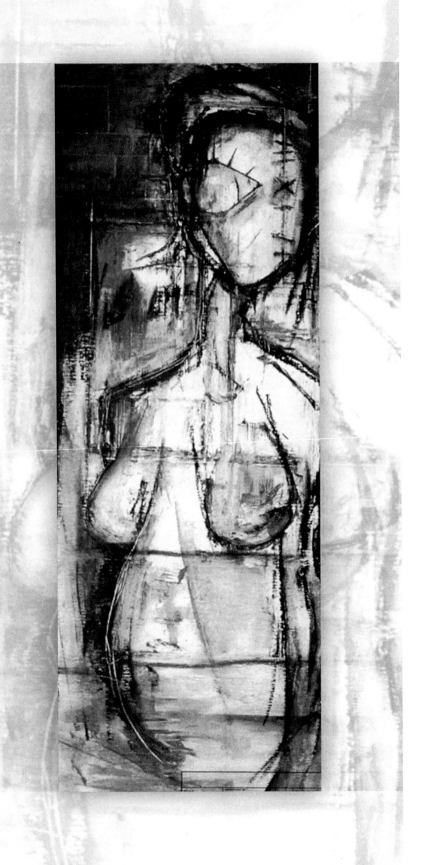

ANGELA

Your love is the epitome
Of all the sustains me
In the wake of what I have become
Now that the weight of my life has succumb
To a will that is greater than my own,
One that has the power to atone
My heart to its utmost content
So that the lingering resentment
Of my often troubled past
Can knowingly, and at long last
Find permanent convalescence
In the warmth of your essence
That, by its very name,
Makes me an orphan without shame.

-R. Douglas Jacobs
June, 2006

Dedicated to Angela Maria Ortiz

PROVIDENCE

Lay unto me your crown of thorns

So that the blood of your scorn

May cleanse me of all sin

And make my spirit akin

To the divine image of your grace;

For then can my rightful place

Within your heavenly domain

Be one that can eternally sustain

My faith in any given form

In order to transform

The toll of my sacrifice

Into a covenant that can suffice

Those whose mourn for loss

Enkindle the sanctity of your cross.

-R. Douglas Jacobs
December, 2004

FERTILE GROUND

Amassed along our vast, nomadic plane

Are furrows that contain

The ancestral remnants of those

Whose lives continue to decompose

For reasons that only nature can shed

Given that the blood with which they bled

Has since vanished beneath

The parched, yet sullied wreath

That solemnly lay to rest

The sins we come to harvest

Once our hearts take root

In being able to salute

A land that our steps will always inter

So that others may live as we were.

-R. Douglas Jacobs
October, 2006

THE IDES OF LAMECH

We die no sooner than we live

Given that we are vindictive

When confronted with the fact

That our tendency to exact

Retribution on any scale

Is no less a biblical tale

Than our birthright

That speaks more of our plight

Then that which we yield

Until the fate that is sealed

Is not that of our own

But one that is known

To fade under the merciless sound

Of a dichotomy abound.

-R. Douglas Jacobs
March, 2007

ELYSIAN FIELDS

Have you ever seen the moonlight
Chase the endless plain of a lonely night
Beyond the reaches of the furthest star?
For you would not have to look far
To discover that the celestial traces
Exists within the ordinary faces
Of those who most surely know
Given that their eyes are aglow
To a pageantry of wonder
That transcends what we see a yonder
Once the fervent gist of their souls
Magnificently arise to extol
The legends that are embolden
In all that is infinite and golden.

-R. Douglas Jacobs
July, 2006

A FINAL RENDERING

To be in search of the perfect verse

Can often be a nagging curse

If I were not so nostalgic

In thinking that the magic

Associated with such an ambitious quest

Is done so at my own behest

So that the sense of truth

I once felt as a youth

Can appear to be heard

As something more than just a written word

Now that my life as a poet

Has made me evermore stoic

To what I knew then

In sharing the wisdom of children.

-R. Douglas Jacobs
July, 2006